{QWERTY}

take my word for it

Andrew Burke

Mulla Mulla Press

QWERTY first published by Mulla Mulla Press, 2011
94 Killarney Street, Kalgoorlie, Western Australia 6430
www.mullamullapress.com

Cover design: Coral Carter
Cover painting: Ross Bennett

Library of Australia Cataloguing-in-Publication entry

Author: Burke, Andrew, 1944-

Title: Qwerty : take my word for it / by Andrew Burke.

Edition: 1st ed.

ISBN: 9780987077127 (pbk.)

Dewey Number: A821.3

For Jeanette

'Come in,' she said, 'I'll give you
Shelter from the storm.'

Bob Dylan

CONTENTS

AS WE ARE

Before he drives off, my friend asks,
'Do you remember desperate times?'

All day, so much speech, so little
meaning, parallelisms on rhetorical
bars. 'I am adjustable,' say the shorts'
monologic care tag. As we are.
Adamson to Creeley, 'These days
we're just words away from death.'

Here I play my lexicon kit, constructing,
melodic, breath and tongue whistling
above the rattle-tattle of my bones.

GROOVES

On hard rock ridges in The Kimberley—
red flushed cheekbones on an ancient face—
grooves scar the surface
where Jaru sharpened their spears.
Wild extremes of weather
haven't worn these stones flat,
millennia haven't erased the patina
of one civilisation before another,
the one before us now.

In my mind I feel grooves
of dogma, prayers and chants,
and the delicious incense
of candles snuffed after Benediction.
Torrential rains have questioned them,
wild winds proved weaker than their hold.
At night in the yard I stand, evaluating
their mark, their meaning,
and turn away
                    unsatisfied.

AFTER TIME

Time takes away after
it has given. The steep sloping
street. Tall house, blue river below,
rock crabs nibbling the shore.

Dog chased the milkman,
Father chased the dog.
You hid in the walk-in
wardrobe and watched

Mother put her face on
in stockings and long-ribbed
bras, then brush away light-brown
from her white upper breasts.

In teenage lovers, Mother jumped
up like jack-in the-box. Someone
took the dog away to a farm …
There was no farm. You realised

time takes away what has
been given. In your dream
dog chased Father until Mother
sprang out the letterbox.

WHITEBAIT

Whitebait, those tiniest sliver
of silver words, swim into
my mind from dark nights
when Mother would feed
the surprise guest brought home
by Father with one too many
drinks in him. Many times
they would mumble apologies
while mother speared a tin
of King Sound whitebait
and started toast cooking.
Father brought home men
who had caught his ear
at the yacht club or the
Naval & Military Club:
an American film actor,
a CSIRO scientist, a touring
Italian pianist, a war hero
with tin legs. Mother would
heat whitebait slowly in
a cream sauce, and when
the toast popped-up (we had
a modern kitchen), she would
say, *Sit down, sit down,*
and all the whitebaits' eyes
would look-up at
my father and his guest
swaying like sailors
just come ashore.

SHOP LOCALLY

'Keith the Butcher is better suited
to conduct my funeral than
Father Fahey,' Frank said in
the shopping centre café, coffee tasting
like burnt tar, muffin crumbling
on his off-white face.
Mock-stained-glass windows framed
consumers relieving aching backs
and knotted veins. 'None of that God stuff
when they send me off, mate.
Dead's dead.' I forewent
a second cup, mentally ticked
off my list, threaded fingers through
handles of Coles supermarket bags,
and stood to go. 'See ya, mate.'
'Not if I see you first.'

In the car park, shopping propped
against the back bumper, I clicked
'unlock', threw open the boot,
and paused, considering the metaphors
of everyday, cryptic tropes of our living
tongue wriggling in the minds of
late capitalist man. 'Hot enough for
you?' asked the woman with
The Goddess Dances on her rear window.

SHOPPING CENTRE GENIUS

"the nothingness of human matters"
- de Man quoting Rousseau

How many suburban shopping centres
have I walked, only to see you
in the eyes of the man
who wanders rootless by himself,
torn summer t-shirt and hooded
winter jacket. He isn't you

yet I see you in his faulty
step forward, hear you in his
every jumbled phrase
in a patois of too many pills
and sleepless nights. Bored,

security guards nickname him
Socrates or The Professor, then offer him
the door, bowing, mock courteous
in their security.

They let you out yet locked you in,
didn't they. Where once you debated
the de Man question, now your day begins
in a chemical blur through shrubbery
sous rature in manicured gardens.

HAVE A NICE DAY

Driving to the shopping centre,
Bukowski rambling in my ear,
I'm glad to be sober
and anonymous. When I was
young, all hormones and energy,
my poetic was all about
getting a fuck. Today I step
from my Toyota, head full
of Buk, and grab a trolley, swearing
at its bent wheels. That'll help,
my sober brain puts in, sarcastic
as ever. I push and the old desire
to be listened to comes back
and I'm impatient at each counter,
waiting for this, waiting for that.
They've got machines now,
not people. Just key in
your late mother's hat size
and, *voila,* the money is out
of your account and into theirs,
Messrs Coles and Woolies. Warmly
I remember the décolletage of
Sandy with the metal in her nose,
tongue and ears. Where is she today?
At the scrap metal yard?
This machine doesn't rock my world.
It doesn't have Sandy's knowing smile,
asking sweetly through banded teeth,
Any fly bys? It's a drive-by, fly by,
bye-bye whirled. Who'll enjoy
fly bys on my funeral plan?
Buk's buggered my mood, but he's

dead and I'm still here, so
who's to complain. The machine
says, *Have a nice day* with
a metallic twang and I
kick the trolley straight again.

A DAY IN THE LIFE

My chest clenches
and I fumble in my pocket
for the Nitrolingual spray.

I'm walking
my damaged heart and dog
through tall gums.

You can watch so much
television, you can nap
just so many hours

then you itch
to do things, simple things
like stretch your legs

and walk.
I stand under a tree
to catch its breath.

A Nitrolingual mist
is working its way
through dank slums

to open the way ahead.
Zimmy sits at my feet, tongue
hanging like

a flag at half mast.
'Come on,' I say,
'let's go.'

HOME FROM HOSPITAL

5am
that silent
time before dawn,
a kookaburra sings solo
outside our courtyard.

On the windowsill
my old comb lies,
clogged with dog's hair.

Time is a measurement of change.

More kookaburras sing now,
like all the canned
laughter of TV's sit coms
played out of control.

I sit at the kitchen table
(I have measured my life
in kitchen tables)
attempting to write
a punch line before
the penultimate break.

SNAP DRAGONS

snap dragons
swaying in
a childhood garden

continue to
snap here
in my old mind

RESPONSE

is tail-feather
and rather not

is line and length
and over

is why the grin
and vicious

is all the above
and doubtful

is drown the sorrow
and hateful

is tell it well
and sickness

is all the apes
and creation

is the final fear
and going on

FACTORY LIFE

At Arctic Coldstores, we called him Bill,
The Box-biting Bastard of Ballarat.
The Dutch foreman was Andy
he'd wave his fists and say, 'I'm 'andy
with these too!' We laughed
coz he was the foreman, but he had
more moods than a chameleon.

I escaped to the attic up a steel ladder—
cold at night, too hot at midday.
My role: to release
ammonia to the freezer rooms.
Down there they wore big black ape suits
to bear the cold, while above them
I sweated like a boy
on his first promise. I'd turn
the wheels sticking up from an inlet pipe
with great difficulty—ammonia
had frozen it to the pipe.
The far one was a bastard
it needed a metal bar wedged
in its wheel to get loose. I chanted,
fuckin' bastard, stupid cunt of a thing,
trying to be one of the boys.

Why wasn't I happy to be a human being?

'Hey, you finished up there, you useless bastard?'

THE OPTHALMIC PROSTHETIST

Back then
I shared an office with
an ophthalmic prosthetist.

Rows of eyes,
dusted with a fine white powder,
stared everywhere.

He himself had
a masterpiece in one socket,
an eye for a dollar in the other.

With his checked sports jacket
knife edge pleated slacks
and clouds of after shave,

he was the original
slick dick—his favourite
hangout, the Happy Haven.

What the whores thought of him
I have only his bragging to tell …

Sometimes, as a laugh,
he would wear a blue eye
and wink with his hazel one.

waking

The inbox and con-
tact lists peep-
holed by
all in

sundry bodies woo-
ing morning
lit lust pre-
sent

and past layers of
liner notes mo-
ving through
bars

intelligent rev-
erance taut
satin on
thigh

white rabbit in a
vegie patch no-
sing the voo
doo

down

BREAKFAST NOWHERE SPECIAL

Greasy spoon breakfast in
a wintry café at dawn. We play
dark corners, coastal cities, outback
towns, by the perennial park where
the war memorial stands and the homeless
drink. A bleak life with scant reward —
they're escaping the nine-to-five,
the rat race, just like us. We play
post-bop, progeny of Miles and Trane,
Elvin and Monk — now we're shrinking
into our Aussie skins, mumbling
smoky echoes, Phoebe with us,
androgynous, on edge, in
catsuit and wig. George reckons
she's a guy, and Jean Paul is
writing her into a suite. We're
coming down over beans and bacon
tipping whiskey into our tea when
the guy's not looking. shades hide our eyes
where smoke and stage lights
leave bleeding tracks. Our
next stop is regional, a cultural centre
built for ballet and opera now needing
funds. Cash is always popular.
'Yeah! Salt peanuts! Salt peanuts!' Paul sings,
slapping the table and we all laugh.
We want the world to know
we were cooking last night,
we were *someone* up there. Now, here,
paradiddling in a dreary
country town dawn
We hang out to keep
The dream drumming.

HAPPY HOUR

Rock faces of Tai Bai Mountain
are stained from ink
Li Bai threw away in rage.

Now Adamson writes
of Mallarme's first drafts
as a squid squirts black ink in his boat—

meaning and faith are
two squirts of brain ink drying
on the wings of fantasy.

This page burns in autumn light.

I'm thinking this one out
behind bottles of Quink
lined up like cocktails on a bar.

KNUCKLE BONES

Of course, things change. In boarding school change was regular: Tuesday and Friday. And the roster for altar boys changed each week. Mass stayed the same, a constant in Latin, but we had a variety of priests, and among them a Hungarian, a refugee without English, whose accent refreshed the Mass. Things do change, don't they, even dogma is different.

When I change, it surprises me.

Once, at what young age I can't recall, I rejected a set of plastic knucklebones as a game, yet later, say two years later or less, I sun-dried bones out from the garbage and empty lots to make my own set of knucklebones. Arthritis came first to my knuckles, the same knuckles I punched in frustration against an office wall, working in a department store, selling goods marked up by too much per cent, paying for the first meals of my first born. Fish oil helps me write now, knuckles flexing over a qwerty keyboard. There is a cricket umpire, Billy Bowden, who has a strange calligraphy of signals for fours and sixes. My mind returns to the Hungarian priest when Billy holds up his arthritic fingers, hooked in the sky as he signals a six. Some in the crowd snigger at his movement whereas my dramatic young mind would have it that the refugee's fingers were distorted by torture in Budapest yet still held Christ aloft so lovingly.

Things change but in my mind small lanes run, a labyrinth, a maze.

PERHAPS

Too much is spoken about illness and medical procedures, too much read into every twitch as sand gathers in the hourglass base.

We sit sipping coffee, mine black for its antioxidant properties, beside young mothers sitting at the next table, prams parked beside their chairs and their babies in their arms, babies wrapped against the autumn breeze in the café courtyard. They are fashionable women, attractive, wearing stylish black and grey, highlighting the white of their breasts as they bare them to feed their babies only weeks old. I am distracted from our talk of travel insurance and such hiccups of aging, distracted not as a young man might be by the beauty of these breasts but by the concept of our lifecycle. Sages are often depicted as old and white-haired with beards flowing down beyond their thorax. Perhaps I know why, perhaps it takes time to ponder things objectively, without the surge of blood, without the wind whistling through wild oats. There's a lot of 'perhaps' in the thinking of an amateur philosopher. I stand and walk back into the café to order another coffee, just to break my thinking, just to get back on track.

PROSE POETRY POEM

'You call that a poem?! I don't call that a poem.' A national flower in one country is a weed in another. 'That's prose.' Would it help if I told you the French started this in modern times? 'The French?! After what they did!' No, before what they did. (May Gertrude press your tender buttons.) The seed grew in the Left Bank of Parnassus, blossomed all around the world, soil on its roots in ancient texts, tendrils running in European breath until *Make it New!* coloured the New World and imagery burst into sunlight, delight. 'Give us a break, Andrew, you've been sold a pup!' A pup digging holes back to its roots. Mind the geraniums, watch the nasturtiums abound willful and free.

ANGIOGRAM

'Don't lift your head! Don't move your arms.' A junior nurse covered the enquiring Robotic Head with a plastic cap. 'Now I'm going to pin your arms beside your sides.' She smiled insincerely. A Japanese face at the door: 'Will I scrub now?' 'Yes,' shouted Dominatrix. I expected a mop and bucket in one hand, a tough-teethed scrubbing brush in the other. Not so: she returned with a colourful surgeon's cap on, a wrap-around apron. 'Don't lift your head!' 'Sorry.' More white ceiling meditation, Om. A small hand lifted the covers on my sexagenarian flanks and swabbed thighs and groin with antibacterial fluid, splashing drunkenly like Pollock in a mood. Colourful cap said, 'A little prick.' Who she referred to I don't know—I was distracted from my meditation by a small pain in my right groin. 'A sting' and it stung. She began steering the Head like an inquisitive praying mantis, testing angles on my chest. I expected to hear, *'Warning! Warning! Aliens approaching!'* and smiled to myself and the white ceiling. The Head flew in close and nudged my shoulder as it took a close up of the cave within. Stalactites and stalagmites competed for room, having grown neighbourly for 65 years. Ceiling fluorescents flicked off, a whirring sound, then blazed again. The Head drew away at speed and swiveled in the purified air, sniffing out some morsel, and bent its neck to peer up-close at my left ribs. They shrunk back in fright. 'Keep still!' a disembodied voice whispered in a stage whisper. 'Last photo,' colourful cap kindly added. She leant down to my ear, 'You have four blockages and …' She spoke on. I lifted my head …

It was so high tech, and such a team of specialists in the control room, theatre and recovery ward, that the final token of the morning's procedure was a deflating surprise. 'Nurse, it may need a band-aid.'

DIARY: ROYAL PERTH HOSPITAL 2010

I am Bed 6GC
beside the helipad.

Identity band on
they won't lose me
I'll know who I am.

There's a ghost of myself
on this bed's TV—
star of my memories.

My daughter brings
Rolling Stone, National Geographic,
this page for
these thoughts.

My right leg, groin and chest
are shaved—skin white

I shower
put stockings on

Helicopter lands
a well-wrapped
lump of humanity—
man, woman or child—
is drawn from its belly.

Pilot has a cup of tea.

5.30am operation day
Nurse Uwe wakes me.

I'm in a hospital gown,
arse hanging out,
bow tied behind my head.

I wait for pre-med. I'm not nervous
yet. Six months since
my heart's silent ambush.

Christ and his two thieves
left their crosses
at the cathedral next door:

weatheredconcrete,
not a splinter on them

It's just a story,' the chaplain says.
'You should know that, Andrew.'

I grew up with Christ's thorns
tattooed on my brain.

When Veronica wipes away my
wounds,
all pain will join the clouds

gathering for this day
When the orderly collects me
he is tall, an urbane African.

We speak of cross-
rhythms and syncopation.

He humours
my nervous prattle

as he pushes my bed down corridors
into lifts to theatre.

The operating team
wear theatre costumes
but the spotlight is on me.

My Greek chorus
leans in leans out,

the room waves
fades to
black.

Day Two

Brittle bones, rechanneled
blood and flawed heart,
I am drained of much
and live in echoes.

My faded book
whispers
of a bleak end.

Day Three

In ICU
logic is off its chain:

I am reduced to tears
as machines measure
ebb and flow of
days, nights worse
as choppers drop
squads of para-
noia troops—terrorists
attack through tubes
into the interior night
shadows of my brain,
a mind field. I am
reduced to fears.

US fast food outlet streets blaze
with orange and red strip neon lighting
flaring like over-exposed video images blazing
into tropical wet fields of Vietnamese farmers
and smoky Chinese street vendors

chopper-mounted machinegun's manic rat-
a-tat-tat rips through
a happy jingle …

nightmare montage

Ward 6G

Late night, I watch
the 2010 Wimbledon Men's Final
Day Four after CABG surgery.
6 to 5 second set,
Nadal has control.

A woman in
the crowd has
my mother's hat on
last worn when
Rod Laver won the Cup.
Nadal and I aren't finished yet—
athleticism and technique will
see us through—*taking the pace off*

his backhand has given him the edge.
Ace. *Nice mixture.*

The runner–up: Tomas Berdych!
Audience applauds wildly.
Obese Bed K2 farts robustly,
Bed K4 snores to wake the dead.

It hurts to laugh
so I share silently
with my mother.

Now, late Night 4, I hug
an outsize scapula to my chest
containing ECG leads
and some connection to
childhood beliefs.

Day Five

Dawn
I walk the Ward.

I'm 'me' again
a paranoid wreck in

the high office of
the individual.

Don't tell them anything.
(imagine telling them that …)

I keep my eye on the Exit sign.

Acknowledgements

Top of the list, Coral Carter of Mulla Mulla Press for publishing this chapbook. Lots of poets mumble angrily that there should be more poetry publishers, but Coral put her money where her mouth is.

Many thanks to Australian artist Ross Bennett for the use of his painting ***Morning*** as a cover image.

While some of these poems are still wet on the canvas, a few have appeared in other places. I thank their editors here:

Response and *waking* were first published at www.frankshome.org and subsequently appeared in Truck Poetry Magazine at www.halvard-johnson.blogspot.com.

Factory Life was first published in Perth Poetry Club's chapbook Positively Geared Anti-TaxPax 2010.

Happy Hour was first published in Brief Magazine *(NZ).*

Snap Dragons is the most visited page on my blog www.hispirits.blogspot.com.

Also by Andrew Burke:

Let's Face the Music & Dance (Peter Jeffery)
On the Tip of my Tongue (Fremanle Arts Centre Press)
Mother Waits for Father Late (Fremantle Arts Centre Press)
Pushing at Silence (SALT Publishing)
Whispering Gallery (Sunline Press)
Knock on Wood (Picaro Press)
Beyond City Limits (International Centre for Landscape and Language at Edith Cowan University)
Mother Waits for Father Late – Revised (Picaro Press)